MW00615673

UNDERSTANDING

GUILT

DURING

BEREAVEMENT

BOB BAUGHER, PH.D.

Table of Contents

Copyright © 2009 by Bob Baugher, Ph.D.

Some Comments Before You Read This Book

Someone you love has died or you are helping a bereaved person and you have picked up this book as a way to work on issues of guilt and grief. Good for you. You are entering a safe place. One of the most difficult issues in the bereavement process is guilt. It is important to understand that guilt has a function and is therefore a common part of the bereavement process. Consequently, you will not see the following words anywhere else in this book: "Don't feel guilty." Go ahead and feel whatever you feel. Not all bereaved people feel guilty. However, the very fact that you are reading this says that you wish to work on your guilt.

That is where this book can help. It will not necessarily take away your guilt; but it will enable you to look at guilt, perhaps more deeply than you ever have before. During the past two decades I have worked with hundreds of people who have experienced the death of a loved one and I have come to realize that an increased understanding of bereavement reactions can help people more effectively cope with their loss.

The 42 contributors to this book have all experienced the death of a loved one through accident, homicide, suicide, or chronic illness. Each has known guilt during bereavement and their combined wisdom, along with research by professionals, helped make this book a reality.

Guilt can be seen as existing on a continuum from unhealthy guilt to healthy guilt. While there is no clear dividing line between the two, this book will give you additional insight into your own guilt by investigating the various dimensions of guilt in the bereavement process through description and example.* The final section will describe suggested methods for coping with guilt. If you are tired

---

*Note: All stories contained in this book have been modified to preserve confidentiality. Some have been taken from published studies, which are designated by brackets [ ] and are referenced at the end of the book.

of being held so tightly by the reins of grief, then some of the suggested ideas might be helpful. Feel free to mark up this book, circling, underlining, and writing comments to yourself.

Guilt is hiding in the grief closets of many bereaved people. The purpose of this book is to open the door and air out your closet. Let's begin by looking at the definition of guilt on the next page.

Definition of Guilt

One definition of guilt is *"Remorseful awareness of having done something wrong."*[1] For the purpose of this book, I will revise the definition to read *"Remorseful awareness stemming from a **perception** of having done something wrong or failing to have done something."* The word perception has been added to the definition of guilt because it doesn't matter whether the bereaved person was actually guilty of wrongdoing. All that matters is that the individual has a self-perception of guilt.

This is why it is difficult to talk someone out of guilt. Think about the last time you encountered someone who stated their guilt feelings, even though you believed them to be innocent. If you demonstrated your logic to them and concluded with, "Therefore, you shouldn't feel guilty," did the person show a change of mind and say, "Yes, you're right. I don't feel guilty now"? Of course not! Once a person begins to travel down the path of guilt, it is usually not easy to turn around.

In his book [2] philosopher Albert Esser sees guilt as a discrepancy between the ideal self and the factual self. Consider this: part of the work on our bereavement is to eventually find ways to feel a little better about yourself—to find a sense of peace.

Esser concludes that there are only five possible reactions to guilt:
1. Forgetting or ignoring
2. Resignation
3. Defiance
4. Regret
5. Repentance.

Esser feels that repentance (a feeling of remorse for past conduct) is the only appropriate response. However, some people who react to guilt during their bereavement may find their most appropriate method for coping is one of the other four listed above. We all have our own style of grieving and it is important to respect the differences.

Turning guilt around isn't easy; but it is possible. The first step is to identify guilt in your life. Putting a name to the various aspects of guilt is a way to begin to work on it. In this book we will identify guilt in four ways:
1. Discover the ways guilt is related to other grief reactions
2. Examine dimensions of guilt
3. Delineate types of guilt
4. Look at the process of guilt

Following this, we will look at suggestions for coping with guilt.

How is Guilt Different from (and Similar to) Other Grief Reactions?

As you read about each of the terms that follow: **Shame, Embarrassment**, **Regret**, and **Anger**, keep in mind that all of them have some degree of relationship to guilt.

Shame

Shame is the result of an event that brings dishonor, disgrace, or condemnation. Death may bring feelings of shame mixed with guilt. For example, a woman whose husband is shot and killed by police during his commission of a burglary may feel ashamed of the way he died and guilty that she was not aware of his illegal activity. Shame is partly based upon our perception of what others think of us.

Looking back on what she felt when her baby died at birth, a mother stated:

> I lost all sense of worth, felt useless and had no confidence in anything I did. Most of all, I now know I never felt worthy of giving myself any praise. I felt a failure and I tried to carry on as normal to compensate for failing everyone else. [3]

In this instance the mother may not have correctly identified her reaction as *shame*. Because grief elicits such a confusing array of emotions, it is common for a person to have difficulty sorting out feelings. [4]

Embarrassment

If we are embarrassed we feel self-conscious or ill at ease. Some bereaved people who feel guilty report feeling highly self-conscious about the circumstances surrounding the death. This may be especially true if they believe that they did something to contribute to the death, or believe they could have done something to have prevented the death. Some family members whose loved one died by suicide report feelings of guilt, shame, and embarrassment.

Regret

Regret happens when a person feels distress over an unfulfilled desire or an action that should or could have been performed or not performed. Much of the guilt that people feel is related to regret. Statements such as "I should've," "Why didn't I?" and "If only . . ." are examples of the regret component of guilt.

Anger

In her book [5] Therese Rando points out that anger is a natural response to being deprived of something valued. Guilt and anger are two of the most powerful grief reactions in the human experience. In addition, anger is related to the third of the five guilt reactions noted by Esser: defiance. For instance, a person coping with guilt-related bereavement may become increasingly disagreeable and obstinate. It may be his or her way of coping with guilt feelings.

During the year following the death of his father from AIDS, eleven year-old Timmy changed from a cooperative fifth grader to an angry and defiant sixth grader. By working with the school counselor, Timmy and his mother began to understand the connection between the tremendous guilt, shame, and embarrassment he was carrying and his acting-out behavior.

Sometimes anger and guilt become intertwined into a vicious circle. The bereaved person who feels guilty is likely to feel self-anger for his or her real or imagined sins. This self-anger can spill onto other people, causing more feelings of guilt, self-anger, and possibly the defiance reactions discussed above. Thus, guilt can cause more anger, which in turn can lead to increased feelings of guilt, leading to more anger, and so on.

An example of this is when Timmy said to his counselor, "After I yelled at my teacher, I felt bad about it. And then I yelled at my friends. This made me feel even worse. It was like I put myself in a trap I couldn't get out of."

Dimensions of Guilt

Let's look at guilt from five different points of view:
Emotional, **Spiritual**, **Cognitive**, **Physical**, and **Behavioral**.

Emotional Dimension

As humans, we experience a complex array of emotions. Guilt is one of them. The key feature of this dimension is that guilt is a *feeling*. Pastor Dick Gilbert said it well, "Feelings are filters. They are the stuff between the outer world and you. It is important to look at what you are feeling so that you can see a new day." [6]

Because there is no such thing as a wrong emotion, it is OK to feel anything, including guilt. People who say to you, "Don't feel guilty," are essentially saying, "Don't *feel*." Since we cannot easily stop ourselves from feeling, it follows that well-meaning friends and relatives cannot take away our guilt. It is up to us to look at it, feel it, understand it, and then see what we might do about it, which is what this book is all about. For example, in the book *The Hole in Me Since the Day You Died* [7], a bereaved mother whose two sons died in infancy, stated:

> [I've been] waiting for someone to come and save me—you know, my husband, my mother, my friends, anyone. I am finally to the point where I know that I am the only one who can help myself.

Spiritual Dimension

For some people, the death of a loved one brings them closer to God or other higher power. If they believe in God, they feel reassured by their belief that their loved one is with God and that God will comfort them in their grief. For others, death is a challenge to their spiritual and religious beliefs. The questioning of why God would take our loved one away can prompt feelings of guilt, anger, and confusion. Prayers that fail to spare a life can lead to a distancing from one's spiritual beliefs. A minister whose wife died of cancer struggled with the guilt he felt over his disappointment that God did not fulfill the prayer requests of his

6

family and entire congregation. Another man whose wife also died of cancer said to me just after her funeral, "The priest said that we were here today to celebrate. I wanted to stand up and say, 'That's not at all why I'm here.' I guess I feel a little guilty for not believing more."

In summary, the Spiritual Dimension has four areas related to guilt:
1. Guilt over unmet expectations that spiritual beliefs would bring comfort
2. Guilt over disappointment that prayers were not answered
3. Guilt over questioning God's love
4. Guilt over lost faith.

Cognitive Dimension

This dimension involves the activities inside our head, including how we perceive the world around us. Four examples related to guilt are: **Guilt Statements, Obsessions, Schema,** and **Selective Perceptions.** Let's take a look.

Guilt Statements

An important way to examine guilt reactions is to list some of the statements that people make when they feel guilty. These first four statements are direct admissions of guilt, while most of the others are regrets of things done or not done; and the last few are more focused on self-punishment.

Look at the list below and note which ones apply to you:
> I feel guilty (or responsible).
> It's my fault -- I'm to blame.
> I neglected someone (or something).
> I did something wrong.
> Something is eating away at me.
> I feel dirty inside.
> If only I…
> Why didn't I…
> I should have…
> I shouldn't have…

Why wasn't I…
I didn't take the time to…
I wish I would've…
This was payback for…
I did everything I could, but I still failed.
It should have been me.
I don't deserve to…
I'm not worthy of…
I should be punished because...

Such statements, also called self-talk or inner dialogue, may be spoken aloud or you may have thought them. As we will see later, negative self-talk is one way that bereaved people punish themselves.

Obsessions

Obsessions are recurring thoughts, which become unhealthy when they disrupt a person's life. When a tragedy occurs, it is common for our brain to review the events over and over and over for days and weeks—sometimes longer. This may happen when various parts of our brain cannot believe that the tragedy is real. So we keep coming back to the events again and again until they finally take hold. Any of the statements in the previous section can become obsessive thoughts.

In some cases people report intrusive images that bring up guilt feelings. For example, Vince saw his brother die in a boating accident and reported re-experiencing the scene, including his failure to save him. Ken, whose son died in a car accident, has imagined himself saying over and over, "Be careful" - something he did not do- before his son walked out the door. Tanya, a 16 year-old girl, says she often hears this in her head, "Why didn't you tell your mother, 'I love you' before she died?" (Later, on page 38, we'll discuss a technique that helped these people, called "Thought-Stopping.")

Guilt Schema

The term schema refers to a cluster of related ideas stored in the brain. For example, we all have a gender schema in which we have stored one set of behaviors more common to males and another set more common to females. When we meet a new person, involuntarily our gender schema leads us to begin making sense of the behaviors of that person in terms of their perceived gender.

Our schemata help us become highly efficient at processing information in our environment. However, our schemata fail us when our daily lives are brimming with guilt. For instance, prior to the death of our loved one, a comment from a friend or a scene on television would have passed without notice. Now, anything can trigger our guilt schema. Death by suicide can create a significant guilt schema. Any hint in conversation of self-harm, giving up on life, or using a particular method (hanging, drugs) can activate intense guilt feelings. The suggestions, beginning on page 30, can help reduce the effect of the guilt schema to a manageable level.

Selective-Perception: Guilt Rewriting History

In his book [2], Alfons Deeken discusses philosopher Max Scheler's insightful thoughts on guilt. Scheler states,

> If anybody should say, 'I am not conscious of any guilt in myself, therefore I have nothing to repent' -- he [or she] must surely be either God or an animal.' (p. 163-4).

In other words, guilt is common to all humans. In addition, Scheler delineates between two modes of time, in relation to guilt. First, objective time is time measured by the clock, as it always moves forward from present to future. Next is human time, which has the capacity to move forward and backward. Therefore, our past is forever uncertain, a constant reprocessing, reformulating, reappraising. In other words, guilt is a way we attempt to rewrite history. We look at the past and selectively perceive events. We continuously review the *what-ifs*—what if I had done this or said that—perhaps this death would not have happened.

In agreement with Esser, Scheler felt that repentance is the key to easing guilt we feel about our past:

> *Repentance conquers the moral evil of the past, brings renewal and rebirth to the present, and works joyfully for a better future. In this way repentance is the most revolutionary force in the moral world. (p. 164).*

What this tells us is that the guilt you have been feeling is a normal process your brain needs to go through. You know the brutal truth: your loved one has died. Nothing can change this fact. However, your brain must find a way to integrate your past behaviors with the fact that you can do nothing to undo the past.

This discrepancy between what you want to do and what you can do creates a gaping hole and a sense of helplessness. Since we do not like the helpless feeling, our brain searches for something we *can* do. So we fill this huge hole with guilt. For some people, feeling guilty may be a way to believe that they can gain some control over the random events in their life. This is one of the functions of guilt. In summary, guilt, repentance, and all the accompanying behaviors noted in this section are normal responses following the death of a loved one.

Physical Dimension

Guilt is carried in our body. At times you may feel it moving through your body. Stop for a moment and answer this question: where in your body do you feel the guilt? Behind your eyes? Deep in your brain? On the back of your neck? On your shoulders? In your heart? In your abdominal area? Guilt is typically described as a heaviness, weighing us down. Conversely, the decrease in guilt is often described as "feeling lighter."

Can we locate guilt in the brain? Something close to it has been identified. It is called the Neuroscience of regret. Because guilt and regret are so closely related, let's look at an interesting finding on regret. Research [8] on the brain has identified an area—called the orbitalfrontal cortex—that appears to house our experience of regret. Two groups of people participated in an experiment in which a gambling session was set up so that, at various times, subjects were told that, had they bet another way, they would have won more money. The group whose orbitalfrontal cortex of the brain had been previously damaged in an accident reported disappointment, but no regret. The group with no history of brain injury to this area of the brain reported disappointment *and* regret. From the results of this study, it appears that regret is wired in to our brain. What this tells us is that we experience regret—and its cousin guilt—whether we want to or not. What we still don't know is why some people experience greater degrees of regret and guilt.

Behavioral Dimension

In this section we will address some of the behavioral outcomes to the previous four dimensions. We'll do this by looking at three identifiable guilt behaviors: **Rituals that Can Become Inflexible**, **Ego Defense Mechanisms**, and **Self-punishment**.

Rituals that Can Become Inflexible

After a loved one dies, it is common to engage in activities that acknowledge that person in some way. This may include:

- Visiting a favorite place
- Going to the place where the person died
- Visiting the cemetery
- Looking at a picture or videos
- Touching or holding an object
- Listening to a song
- Talking to the person
- Taking time out to acknowledge the person in some way
- Working on a project
- Joining an organization

If any of these activities have become something you feel that you <u>must</u> do, then the activity has reached the level of an inflexible ritual. Guilt may occur when you either forget or decide to skip a ritual. Has this happened to you? If so, you may have heaped blame on yourself for getting "too busy" with life and forgetting your loved one. This adds more guilt feelings. After his nine year-old daughter died, Jerome formed a ritual in which he would look at her picture in the hallway just before entering his bedroom. After several months of this, one day he found himself standing in his bedroom. What happened? He forgot to look at his daughter's picture! He panicked. He said, "I stood there, beating myself up, saying, 'What kind of father am I that would forget my daughter?'" Later in the week he hesitatingly shared his story in a parent support group. By doing this, Jerome began to realize that he was feeling guilty for getting better (see page 27) and was assured by the other supportive parents that this step did not in anyway signify that he was forgetting his daughter.

Ego Defense Mechanisms

According to Psychoanalytic Theory, our ego is the sense of self that we carry with us wherever we go. The theory states that whenever we make a mistake, our ego demands that it be defended so that we won't look so bad. Below are examples of the ways that we might defend our ego within the context of guilt.

Scapegoating. This refers to taking one's negative feelings out on an innocent party. An example of this was discussed earlier in the section on Anger (eleven year-old Timmy). The key feature of this mechanism is that the person has feelings of guilt and, instead of admitting it, uses a scapegoat. Typically the scapegoats we choose are those most available to us -- those with whom we come into contact most frequently: relatives, friends, fellow employees. It can also include blaming doctors, police officers, caregivers, and anyone else who was associated with the death. We become more focused on blaming innocent others rather than looking at our own guilt feelings.

Another form that Scapegoating takes is when other people blame us and we feel guilty as a result of their accusations. A mother whose seven year-old son died in an auto accident in which another car clipped the front end of her car causing it to hit a cement overpass described the overwhelming guilt she experienced shortly after she arrived at the hospital emergency room:

After being taken by ambulance to a local ER and treated for my own injuries, I was alone in my ER room with a nurse and a policeman, the ER doctor, the coroner and my ex-husband [my son's father] all at the same time and this is what happened…The policeman tells me that they need to take my blood to do a drug test to make sure that I wasn't impaired while driving… the doctor tells me immediately after that my beautiful son did not make it, the coroner tells me that they need to do an autopsy to ensure that I had not killed my son before I put him in the car and had drove my vehicle into the overpass on purpose to make it look like an accident, and my ex-husband then starts swearing at me and accusing me of "murdering our boy" and lunges at me with his hands around my throat, at which time the doctor, policeman and nurse pull him off of me and escort him out of my room…

Clearly this mother experienced high levels of guilt brought on by the rapid-fire accusations of others.

Undoing. As the name implies, Undoing indicates that the person is trying to rectify a situation after making a mistake. This typically occurs without the offending person apologizing or taking responsibility for their mistake.

For example, following the death of her father in an auto accident in which she was the cited driver, 40 year-old Lisa attempted to sue the auto manufacturer for a faulty steering mechanism. The jury found no evidence for such a claim. Following the court case Lisa sought therapy for her distress. She later admitted to her therapist that she had filed the claim, hoping it would exonerate her and ease her guilt over her father's death. In addition to illustrating Undoing, this scenario also illustrates Scapegoating, as Lisa attempted to shift blame from herself to an innocent party.

<u>Emotional Insulation</u>. Sometimes we don't want to admit to other people what we are feeling. This may be especially true when it comes to guilt. Therefore, some people who have guilt feelings will defend their ego by acting as if they feel no guilt when they actually do. This is related to the earlier discussion of one of Esser's five reactions to guilt: forgetting or ignoring.

A 15 year-old boy urged his 13 year-old brother to pick up a handgun. The gun went off, killing the younger brother. A year later, when the boy joined a youth grief support group, he was asked if he felt any guilt for his brother's death. He stoically said he felt little guilt and stated, "Why am I even here? I'm doing all right." By the fifth week, with care and gentle guidance from the group he had become more comfortable sharing his feelings and admitted experiencing a great deal of guilt about his brother's death. For a few weeks after his admission he reported feeling worse than he ever had since his brother died. As the months went by however, he reported feeling better, "lighter" as he put it.

A precaution on Ego Defense Mechanisms: It is not always possible to determine if any particular individual—such as the case with the 15 year-old boy—is using a defense mechanism. Only later, when a person has gained some perspective on guilt and grief, can it be assessed that the person was defending the ego.

Self-Punishment

Another behavior that may accompany guilt is self-punishment. This often comes from the person's need to somehow "balance the scale" of life events. When we were children, we often received some form of punishment for our misbehavior. This may be one of the ways that children form their conscience. So, even as adults, when we find ourselves in a guilt-producing situation, we may feel a need to receive punishment.

We might exhibit some of the following behaviors:
- Saying negative things to ourselves
- Replaying the perceived mistake(s)
- Depriving ourselves of something.

However, some people feel the need to hurt themselves in significant ways:
- Inflicting some form of bodily pain
- Not eating
- Overeating
- Purposeful public embarrassment
- Failing to engage in self-care, (e.g., personal hygiene, taking prescribed meds)
- Cutting on themselves
- Permitting themselves to fall into harm's way, e.g., reckless driving, not tending to a medical condition
- Getting in a fight in which they know they will be hurt
- Abusing alcohol and/or drugs
- Any form of self-destructive behavior
- Self-isolating
- Suicide attempt

Such behaviors are among the most disruptive for people in the midst of grief. They are related to two of Esser's five possible reactions to guilt: resignation and repentance. In an attempt to "even the score" these individuals believe it necessary to continue their self-destructive behaviors. It can be very difficult to talk an individual out of such behaviors, especially when a person is considering suicide.

However, there is hope. A caring person can be a good listener and help the person get assistance in the form of a support group or counseling. In addition, there are other forms of helpful intervention, which will be discussed in the Suggestions for Coping section on page 30.

Next let's look at types of guilt.

Types of Guilt

(Adapted from Miles & Demi [9])

Another important way to identify your guilt reactions is to understand the various types of guilt that can occur during the bereavement process. Margaret Miles and Alice Demi did some of the early research on six types of guilt in their work with bereaved parents: Death Causation, Illness-related, Role Guilt, Moral Guilt, Survival Guilt, and Grief Guilt. To these, I have added eight more. You may find that some of these overlap with one another. The purpose of this section is to help you identify areas of guilt in your own life. At the end of each guilt type, I've included a reference to one or more of the 22 suggestions that begin on page 30.

1. Death Causation Guilt

This can occur whether or not the person was actually directly responsible for the death. Think of it on a continuum from one extreme to the other, with all the gradations in between.

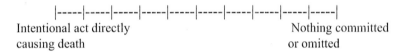

Intentional act directly   Nothing committed
causing death   or omitted

Another way to consider Death Causation Guilt is to view it in steps. Note that the following list is not necessarily sequential:

1. Planned, intentional act leading to the death
2. Unplanned, intentional act leading to the death
3. Unplanned, unintentional act leading to the death
4. Failing to save the person
5. Negligent act leading to the death; failing or forgetting to do something that *clearly* led to the death
6. Doing or not doing something that *may* have led to the death
7. Doing or not doing something that led to the situation in which the death occurred
8. Doing something or failing to do something that any reasonable person would say had no relationship to the death; yet, the person feels responsible.

(See Suggestions #1, 3, 5, 13, 14.)

2. Illness-Related Guilt

In this type of guilt the focus is on the time period prior to and including the illness of a person who later died. The bereaved person may feel guilty for any of the following:

- Not believing the person was ill
- Not noticing symptoms that led to the illness and the death
- Noticing symptoms, but not taking appropriate action
- Not taking proper care of the person during the illness
- Not being able to stop the pain of the person during the illness
- Not intervening on behalf of the person on some issue involving a healthcare professional
- Giving permission for a medical procedure that caused more pain or made things worse
- Not giving permission for a medical procedure that might have resulted in a cure, a longer life, and/or decreased pain
- Not visiting enough during the illness
- Wishing the person dead
- Feeling grateful for not being the one who was ill
- Saying or doing something negative during the illness
- Being resentful or angry at the person for being ill
- Placing the person in a nursing home
- Doing something to prolong the illness
- Doing something to hasten the death

During a nursing home visit with her aunt, 13 year-old Jill [10] was getting ready to leave when her aunt grabbed her hand, looked her in the eyes and said, "You'll come visit me one more time before I die won't you?" Jill replied, "Sure." "Promise?" asked her aunt." "Promise" replied Jill. The next weekend Jill missed the next visit; and of course Jill was devastated when, three days later, her mother called crying saying that her aunt had just died.

An example of guilt over hastening a death is seen in the case of a woman who found herself in the unfortunate position having to give the word to turn off the ventilator that was keeping her husband's body functioning. Despite the fact that the medical team helped her understand that her husband's comatose condition was irreversible, years later, she continues to feel some guilt.

Many of the examples of illness-related guilt are linked to choices grieving people had to make on medical procedures for their loved ones. Were you faced with a myriad of medical choices? After the death did you second-guess yourself, knowing that you *should have* made a different choice? During our lives, we all have had to make decisions based on the best information we had **at the time**. This is also true when we have to make medical decisions based on the available information provided by medical staff. Illness-related guilt comes out when we kick ourselves for making the "wrong decision." At the time, we made the best decision possible. We'll revisit this issue in the next section on Suggestions for Coping with Guilt. (See especially suggestions #5, 12, and 15.)

3. Moment-of-Death Guilt

Were you there when your loved one died? Do you wish you were? Most people do. Unless there is clear warning, we will not be there when a death takes place. But that doesn't stop us from feeling that we should have been there, should have known, and should have somehow realized that the end was near.

Some people report having what they believed was a premonition, a sign, or some indication that "something was about to happen." By not acting on this sensation the person now feels tremendous guilt. Early that morning, when Rob received the phone call from the rehab center telling him that an ambulance was taking his father to the hospital, he reported saying to himself, "Look at the sky. The cloud formations are so strange—like circles." By the time he and his sister arrived at the hospital, he discovered that his father had died en route. Later on, Rob caught himself thinking, "The sky was so different that morning. I should have known something was going to happen. I should have insisted on riding in the ambulance with Dad." Despite the fact that his drive to the rehab center would have delayed the ambulance and the medics had instructed him to go directly to the hospital, Rob insists, "I should have been there with him. He shouldn't have died alone, with strangers."

(Suggestions #4, 5, and 12 may help.)

4. Role Guilt

A role is an expected set of behaviors. When a person we care about dies, guilt may emerge and we may brood over, "what I should have done" with or for this person.

In the book *When a Baby Dies of SIDS* [11] a father states, "What was there in front of my face that I didn't see?"

Here is an example of an adult son's eventual Role Guilt [12]: One day, Jerry, a successful attorney, has a conversation with his father in his father's office. His father said, "Your life has been a total disappointment." Stunned, Jerry responded, "To whom, Dad—you or me?" As Jerry later recalls the story, he laments:

> With that comment I walked out of his office and virtually out of his life. I saw him at family get-togethers, yet a distance existed that could not be bridged. I was well prepared for my father's demise, having dealt with his [stroke]…What I was not prepared for, though, was the effect of having so much left open, unresolved, and hanging in our relationship.

Let's examine the variety of roles in people's lives and the kind of guilt statements they might make.

Parent
"I wasn't a good enough protector."
"I was overprotective."
"I wasn't a good enough provider."
"I gave my child too much."
"I punished him too much."
"I was too permissive."
"I was too restrictive."
"I wasn't a good enough teacher."
"I wasn't a good enough listener."
"I didn't show enough affection."
"I had unresolved issues with my child."
"I passed unhealthy genes to my child."

Grandparent
"I should have been more involved with my grandchild."
"If only I had communicated more with my daughter (or son), this may not have happened."
"I feel so helpless because I cannot take away my son's (or daughter's) pain."

Spouse/Partner
"I wasn't a good enough partner."
"We argued, belittled, yelled, nagged, considered divorce."
"I didn't take the time . . . ."
"I didn't show enough appreciation."
"I took him (or her) for granted."
"I didn't show enough affection."

Sibling
"I was jealous of her."
"I was envious of the attention given to my dependent brother."
"I regret not being closer."
"I'm ashamed to say that I wished he were dead."
"I didn't visit her (enough) during her illness."
"I didn't take time to be with him when he was healthy."

Parent Death
"Her death was because of something I did (or didn't do)."
"I was mean to her."
"I never got to patch up our relationship."
"I hated visiting him when he was sick."
"I never got to make him proud of me."

General Role Guilt
"I've failed to keep the promise I made to him."
"I'm not honoring her wishes."
"I'm doing things that he wouldn't approve."
"I'm not properly remembering or memorializing him."

(See in particular Suggestions #4, 8, 11, 12, 15.)

5. If-Only (or Failure) Guilt

This type of guilt stems from the belief that the bereaved survivor could have done something to have changed the course of the illness and/or death. If only I had:

> Said, "Be careful."
> Said, "I love you."
> Been more strict.
> Not been so strict.
> Noticed the symptoms.
> Kept her here a little longer.
> Gotten a second opinion
> Told him not to do that.
> Done things differently.
> Been less career- and more family-oriented
> Seen this coming.
> Not let pride get in the way.
> Been a better _____.
> Not gotten that for him.
> Watched her more closely.
> Not told her to do that.
> Taught him how to be more careful.
> Not moved to this neighborhood.
> Made her do (or not do) _____.
> Been a better person.

These statements are related to a phenomenon known as *Hindsight Bias*. Once people know the outcome of an event, they tend to overestimate how much predictive information they had beforehand. We've all heard that hindsight is 20-20. But, when a death occurs, especially a sudden death, our mind furiously works backward to scour every conceivable factor that we *should've* noticed. Sound familiar? Hence, we come up with all of our "If-onlys." How many in the list above have you said to yourself?

(See Suggestions #2, 6, 9, 18.)

6. Moral Guilt

Moral beliefs about how we should behave can derive from religious, spiritual, or personal values. Moral guilt is related to two of Esser's ideas of how we react to guilt: regret and repentance. Thus, when a death occurs, moral guilt involves looking back at our life and attempting to derive connections between our past (perceived) sins and the reasons for the death.

Here are some of the statements that may reflect Moral Guilt:
"This death is punishment for his past sin(s)."
"This is a type of karma for past behaviors—what goes around comes around."
"The death is a form of counterbalance for all the good things that have happened in my (or his) life. In other words, I believe that if you have too much good in your life, something bad must happen--like this death--to balance it out. This death is a type of payback for the good that has happened."
"My family is cursed."
"This is punishment from God."

An example of the last two statements comes from the book *The Bereaved Parent* [13] in which a father stated:

When you get married you swear to forsake all others, too. But…I began playing around. Then our son developed cancer. I watched his agony and couldn't handle it. Aside from seeing someone I loved in pain, I began to believe my son—my only boy—was suffering because I had sinned. God was punishing me. When my boy died, I just could not be comforted. Or rather, I would not let myself be comforted because I felt responsible for what happened.

Some people see death as God's way of getting their attention:

I felt like God might be punishing me for not being involved enough with my family, and this was the only way He could get my attention and tell me I needed to devote less time to work and more to family. I felt that if I had realized that my family was the most important, God wouldn't have had to do this to me [14]

Well-meaning people believe they are helping a bereaved person when they use the cliché "everything happens for a reason." For example, the mother mentioned earlier, whose seven year-old son died in an auto accident in which another car clipped the front end of her car, stated:

> A lot of folks say to me "everything happens for a reason" and I cannot come up with any good reason whatsoever [for the death of my son]. So confusion in the spiritual dimension is a huge component of my grief and also adds to the guilt, because I can only land (at this time) on "I must be a terrible mother."

(See Suggestion #19.)

7. Guilt by Proxy

Sometimes a person will "take on" the guilt of another person. It is more likely to happen when the actual guilty party is incapable or unwilling to feel guilt. For example, when a man was apprehended for the murder of his girlfriend, he expressed no overt guilt for his actions. However, his mother carried a tremendous amount of guilt for years afterward—not only for her perceived failure to be a good parent but also because, as she put it, "Someone needs to feel guilty about this." (See Suggestions #3, 14, 17.)

8. Survival Guilt

Sometimes called *Survivor Guilt*, it emerges from the very act of outliving our loved one. This is particularly common with the surviving parents and siblings. It also occurs when one or more persons die but others survive the catastrophe. War is a common example. Common statements are:

"I'm here and he's gone. Why?"

"Why did I outlive her? Why didn't I die first?"

"Every day (every second) I live means I have lived that much longer than him – and that's not right."

"I don't know how to live without her."

"Better people than I have died. Why?"

"This is wrong. A parent shouldn't outlive a child. Never"

After her husband died, a well-known death educator and researcher [15] stated, "I didn't want to eat because he could never eat again. Watching a beautiful sunset seemed selfish, because he would never be able to see one again."

Sometimes guilt emerges when we pass the age of the person who died or when we find ourselves doing things our loved one never got a chance to do.
(See Suggestions #2, 8, 12, 22.)

9. Inducing-Pain-in-Others Guilt

In addition to coping with our own grief, another area of great pain is watching others grieve. If your mother died, you may feel guilty for not being able to ease the pain of your children or your sister or your father. If your husband or wife died, it may pain you to watch his or her parents grieving the loss of their child. The death of a child not only leaves a grieving mom and dad and siblings, but grandparents, aunts, uncles, and cousins. Watching helplessly as these people grieve may lead to a belief that if it weren't for this death, these relatives might be OK.

A bereaved dad pointed out how difficult it has been to watch his parents grieve the death of their grandchild. He stated, "Sometimes I get this crazy thought that if my wife and I hadn't brought our son into the world, my parents and my wife's parents and brother wouldn't be hurting right now."

A related aspect is the guilt felt when one's own grief responses bring pain to others. Knowing that your tears and sadness upset your family members can bring feelings of guilt. Because of this, some people hide their grief.

An 18 year-old college student told me, "When my sister died two years ago, it was so hard for me to see my parents grieve. I know they were concerned about me, so I pretty much didn't cry in front of them and saved it when I was in my room at night."

(See Suggestions #4, 20.)

10. Relief Guilt

When the person who died had caused a great number of problems during his or her life, the death for some people may have been somewhat of a relief [16].

A man shared the story of how much he loved his sister despite her drug addiction and lawlessness. But when she died, he reported feeling guilty about the relief he felt knowing that, "I wouldn't be wondering what she's up to and wouldn't be getting anymore calls at all hours of the night."

In addition, after watching a person suffer for a prolonged period of time may bring feelings of relief when the death occurs. For some people this is not an issue. But some people question themselves, asking, "How can I be so cruel to want this person dead?"

(See Suggestions #13, 15, 20.)

11. Benefit Guilt

When the death of a person we love is followed by a benefit, we may have mixed feelings. For some people, life insurance or a court settlement brings feelings of gratitude mixed with guilt.

A few months after their son's death a couple received notice from an attorney that their son's workers' union carried a $10,000 life insurance policy. Upon receiving the check, the parents were torn with how to use it. They had bills to pay, but felt the check was blood money.

The proceeds of a will may also become a source of guilt. What if the money or inherited property is somehow misused or if one person receives more than their fair share? Or what if a person is given ownership as the result of a death such as when a sibling dies and the surviving brother or sister is given the sibling's possessions? Guilt has a way of creeping into many areas following a death.

(See Suggestions #2, 22.)

12. Grief Guilt

Years ago I wrote an article for Bereavement Magazine [17] entitled, "What If I Grieved Perfectly?" It was a tongue-in-cheek piece in which I invited readers to imagine what their perfect bereavement process would be. It originated from my realization that no one has ever come to me and said, "You know, I'm grieving just right."

With this in mind, look at the sentence and insert each word or phrase from the list of words that follow to see if you recognize any statements that may have contributed to your guilt.
"I'm not _____ enough." Or "I'm _____ too much."

> angry
> sad
> visiting the cemetery
> remembering/thinking of him/her
> feeling bad
> dreaming about him/her
> punishing myself
> grieving

Another example of Grief Guilt is feeling guilty for having angry feelings towards the person who died. As I discussed earlier, this type of anger is more likely to be associated with suicide, but can occur with any form of death.

(See Suggestions #6, 10, 14, 16.)

13. Unmentionable Guilt

Sometimes the guilt a person feels is difficult to discuss because it involves a secret that is believed to be too terrible to utter. It may involve knowledge of things that the person who died was involved in; or it may be something that the bereaved survivor did. In either case it complicates the bereavement process by layering guilt on top of guilt.

Examples of this are:
- Drug or alcohol use
- Dishonesty
- Criminal activity
- Physical, emotional, sexual abuse
- Infidelity
- Information about how the death really occurred

In some cases the bereaved person may have exclusive knowledge of the facts of the death, but for some reason is reluctant to reveal the truth.

If you identify with any of this, please pay special attention to Suggestions #4 and 20.

In the case of a missing person who has yet to be found after a number of years—called Ambiguous Loss [18]—some friends and relatives may quietly withdraw their energy from the search. This can cause high levels of guilt because the bereaved person sees him or herself as giving up. As a result many people in this situation keep their decision to themselves, but carry these unmentionable feelings for years.

14. "Getting Better" Guilt
Getting better does not mean that the person is back to normal. Years after a death bereaved people find themselves at a place in their life different from any they ever experienced or imagined. Their entire world has been altered forever. They are, what many people report, in a "new normal."

This form of guilt is concerned with the times in which the individual realizes that he or she is:
- Living life without his or her loved one
- Feeling good about being alive
- Experiencing pleasure without feeling guilty
- Going through several minutes, or even hours in the day and not thinking about the loved one
- Beginning a new relationship

27

It often happens that months or years after the death the person is involved in an activity and suddenly realizes that he or she is actually feeling better. Or it could be that the person has not thought about the loved one for a time. When this occurs, the person might feel guilt. It may take the form of a panic reaction.

For example, the person may say, "Oh my God, I'm forgetting him!" and may begin to feel the loved one fading from memory. Worse, the person may feel that the forgetting process will progress. The person may say, "I can't believe this. He was in my life. He was my entire life. I loved him. How can I be forgetting him? I won't let this happen!" The person then makes a promise to never again fall into the trap of moving on with life, which yields forgetting. However, the person is now in what can be called "the trap of guilt" that impedes the process of grief. Let's look at two examples.

Guilt Trap #1. An important sign of progression in the bereavement process is reinvesting in life. At the very moment that we begin to feel a little better, our guilt feelings emerge which leads us to conclude that we must be forgetting our loved one. As a result, we "snap back" from our positive feelings and convince ourselves that moving on with life (the very epitome of positive coping with grief) is wrong. Therefore, the only way that we can overcome this guilt trap is to understand that **moving on does not equal forgetting or losing our love for this person.**

Guilt Trap #2. Another trap occurs as the survivor gradually comes to realize that many life goals might never be realized because life has drastically changed. The person is in the following conflict: "If I work on these goals, then I am moving on with my life without my loved one. So why even work on them? Yet, if I put the goals aside, I may regret not having done them. I feel guilty either way."

(See Suggestions #2, 10, 12, 13.)

With the guilt behaviors and guilt types in mind, let's look next at the process of guilt and then examine 22 ways to cope with guilt.

The Process of Guilt

Next, let us move to an analysis of the actual guilt process by asking questions much like a physician uses in diagnosing. If you are marking your answers here or on a separate sheet of paper, I suggest that you include the date so that when you later view your answers, you can see what has changed and what has not.

1. *Frequency*. Are feelings of guilt always present? If not, how often do I find myself experiencing guilt feelings?

2. *Intensity*. When I experience guilt, how intense is the reaction?

a. Barely noticeable	d. Somewhat intense
b. Mild	e. Very intense
c. Moderate	f. Severe—debilitating

3. *Duration*. Once the guilt feelings arise, how long, do they last?

a. Disappear in a second or two	f. For most or all of the day
b. Gone in a few minutes	g. For days
c. More than a few minutes	h. For weeks
d. For an hour or so	i. My guilt feelings never
e. For several hours	seem to leave me

4. *Degree of debilitation*. The degree to which this guilt is debilitating me is:

a. Not at all   b. Slightly   c. Somewhat   d. Quite a bit   e. A great deal

Look back at your answers. You should have an idea of the significance of guilt in your life. Is your guilt frequent, intense, prolonged, and debilitating? If so, this means that you are a good candidate to get some help with guilt. This book can be a start. Refer to the suggestions beginning on the next page and consider talking to a friend, joining a support group, and/or seeing a counselor. Is your guilt and self-punishment standing in the way of talking to another person? Please use the suggestions in this book to help you take a step forward.

Suggestions for Coping with Guilt

What follows are suggestions that may help you cope with your guilt feelings. The 22 suggestions come from bereaved people who have shared with me what has worked for them. These people include bereaved parents, siblings, grandparents, spouses and people whose parents have died. Use suggestions that you feel may apply to you at this time in your life. Working on grief and guilt takes time and is done at your own individual pace. Try the suggestions to see how they work for you.

Some suggestions may be uncomfortable for you. Some involve writing. So please don't just sit and passively read. Pick up a pen and pad or go to your computer and start writing. There is something powerful about getting your thoughts and feelings on paper.

1. Educate yourself

By reading this book you have learned more about the guilt process and realize that:

- Guilt is a normal part of the bereavement process.
- Guilt is similar to, yet distinct from shame, embarrassment, regret, and anger.
- Self-talk is an important element of guilt.
- Guilt has emotional, spiritual, cognitive, behavioral, and physical dimensions.
- You have gained insight into your guilt reactions by filling out the survey.
- There are many types of guilt.

2. Guilt throughout the years: A review

(A suggestion by Sara Weiss)

Fill in the boxes below by considering each type of guilt and its frequency, intensity, and duration. You may want to write the date on this page to see where you are as time goes by. Use the following scale:

30

0=little or no guilt
1=slight degree of guilt
2=some degree of guilt
3=quite a bit of guilt
4=high level of guilt

	Years					
Types of Guilt	0-1/2	1/2-1	1-2	2-3	3-5	5+
1. Death Causation Guilt						
2. Illness-Related Guilt						
3. Moment-of-Death Guilt						
4. Role Guilt						
5. If-Only Guilt						
6. Moral Guilt						
7. Guilt by Proxy						
8. Survival Guilt						
9. Pain to Others Guilt						
10. Relief Guilt						
11. Benefit Guilt						
12. Grief Guilt						
13. Unmentionable Guilt						
14. Getting Better Guilt						

Now that you are finished, take out a pen and paper (or your computer) and write your story of guilt. Although this may be difficult for you, research [19] shows that getting our problems on paper is a critical step in helping us cope with life's problems.

3. Assess your personality tendency toward guilt

For some people, guilt is related to control. What this means is that people who have a high need to control things in their life may feel higher levels of guilt when things do not go their way. Following the death of his daughter, a bereaved dad said this to me, "You know, before all this happened I thought I had control of my life— my job, my family, my world. But now I realize that I don't have much control at all. This grief stuff is a whole new world to me."

Does any of this apply to you? If part of your grief is related to loss of control, I don't have to tell you that your world-view has dramatically changed. You are likely to have a high number of statements that begin with "I should've," "Why didn't I," and "If only." The question to ask yourself is: "Can I let go of these statements?" More about this in Suggestion #18, Setting a Date.

4. Focus on the positive
In their book [9] Margaret Miles and Alice Demi offered a method for reducing guilt: to focus on the positives in the relationship. Take out a piece of paper and quickly write a word, phrase, or sentence for each positive experience that comes to mind.

Here are some questions to guide you:
1. How are you grateful for having had this person in your life?
2. What are examples of events that produced joy and laughter?
3. What brought excitement?
4. Where are places you visited?
5. What things did you teach this person?
6. What things did you learn from this person?
7. How do you treat others as a result of this person's influence?
8. Even if your loved one lived a short life, write examples of all the comfort and caring you gave and all that you received.
9. What has this death taught you?

Please do this now. Later, when you find yourself starting to feel some guilt, bring up this list of positives in your relationship. When I sat with a bereaved mom whose daughter died at age four, and had her answer some of the questions, at first her writing was hesitant; but after a few minutes her writing began to flow, filling up three pages of the positive aspects of her life with her daughter.

An example of question #7 above is found in a five-year follow-up study of parents whose children died from an accident, suicide, homicide, or unknown. Murphy [20] found that the most important factors that helped parents find some degree of meaning in their child's death were re-ordering priorities and gaining a greater appreciation of family and friends.

5. When the death occurred, you were likely doing what you would have normally been doing at the time.
A helpful quote is, "Guilt is putting today's knowledge on yesterday's problems." [21]

We discussed this earlier in the section on Illness-Related Guilt. Guilt rears its head in situations where we were not present. For example, a bereaved mom whose son died in an auto accident said, "I had to eventually come to the point where I could say to myself: You did the best you could at the time. At the time you made the decisions you did with the best information you had."

If, after reading the previous statement, you are saying, "No, I didn't," then please read on. When the illness, accident, homicide, or suicide occurred, what were you doing at the time? When you made a decision that related to the death, you likely made the decision with the best information you had at that time.

It is easy to fall into the Hindsight Bias discussed earlier and look back and say:
> "Why didn't I do it differently?"
> "Why didn't I see what could happen?"
> "I should've known better."

However, right now, can you return back to your life *exactly* as it was back then? First of all, it's difficult, if not impossible to remember your thoughts, feelings, and all that was going on during those days in your life.

Second, if you had been able to predict the future at that point in your life, of course there are things you would have done differently. No one--not even you--can predict exactly what will happen in life. Yet, you continue to blame yourself.

Consider this harsh, but real possibility: Even if you had done things differently, it is still possible that your loved one could have died the very next day from some other cause. I know this may be difficult to imagine, but it is important for you to understand that the guilt about your own perceived contribution to the death can be seen from a different perspective.

Stop for a moment and say to yourself the following words, "What if I had done things differently? Is it possible that my loved one still could have died in some other way the very next day?" You know that the answer is "Yes." However, despite this logic, you may still find yourself going through the "What if's?" again and again.

From now on, can you include in your answer to your guilt questions the following statements?
a. "Even if I had done things differently, my loved one might still have died."
b. "There are some things over which I have *no* control."

Moreover, your guilt may come from what you have learned about yourself following the death. Given that you cannot change the past, can you use your knowledge of guilt to work with who you are now and who you want to be?

We will look into this more deeply in the section on Channeling Guilt (page 48).

6. Self-talk: Addressing the Shoulds and If-Onlys

In their book *Woulda, Coulda, Shoulda* [22] Arthur Freeman and Rose DeWolf discuss our "shoulds" by using the metaphor of riding a horse on a trail 20 feet wide with sheer cliffs on either side. We can enjoy this ride by leisurely staying clear of the cliffs. But, what if the path were only two feet wide? Despite all our best efforts we are bound to make a mistake trying to stay on the narrow path.. The question these authors ask is: "Which path is more representative of your *shoulds*? The wide path? Or the narrow one with its many constrictive rules to which you respond by constantly beating yourself up? Let's look at a couple questions regarding your path of *shoulds*.

Question 1: What are my "Should haves" and "Shouldn't haves"? That is, when you say to yourself, "I should've done something or said something," to what exactly are you referring? If you are writing, please jot down your answer.

Question 2: Do I understand that when I say the words "should have" or "shouldn't have" I cannot actually *do* anything about it? Two examples are: "I shouldn't have yelled at her so much" and "I should have known something like this would happen." The people who said this have regrets, but they can do absolutely nothing about the past. Consider omitting these phrases from your vocabulary and replacing each of them with: "What can I now do?"

"I should have/shouldn't have."	"What can I now do?"
"If only . . ."	"What can I now do?"
"Why didn't I (he or she) . . .?"	"What can I now do?"

A mother whose son died from suicide put it well [23]:

> After all you've read about grief, there will be times that you think you won't or can't make it….It has been ten years since the suicide of our son, Matt. The road is paved with pain and hurt, questions and no answers, silence on the part of many, old friends lost and new friends made. It's a long road—difficult and oftentimes with the feeling of no progress. If you somehow remember the four words, "I can make it," you will.

7. Practice responding to other people

Research on helpful and unhelpful grief support statements [24] found the most <u>unhelpful</u> messages were giving advice and minimizing feelings.

Here are two scenarios in which people say potentially guilt-inducing statements:

<u>Scenario 1</u>: People may give advice that ends up triggering feelings of guilt. For example, two weeks after the suicide of Alexander's 20 year-old brother, his uncle Tony said to him, "Alexander, if you pray hard, your grief will go away."

<u>Scenario 2</u>: People may try to minimize your guilt feelings. For example, a friend of Tuan said, "Why are you feeling so guilty? Your brother chose to pull the trigger. It's been four months. It's time to move on."

A way to handle unhelpful remarks is to write them down. Beside each statement write the most appropriate response in order to be prepared for the next time.

In Scenario 1, the reply could have been, "Thank you, Uncle Tony. But I'm a little mad at God right now. So, give me some time, OK? It'll take as long as it takes."

In Scenario 2, Tuan might have said, "I absolutely know it was his choice to use the gun; but despite this, I still have guilt feelings that need to be dealt with. Thanks for caring."

You might practice your response with a friend.

8. Suggestions for parents

Bereaved parents find it especially difficult to watch their surviving children cope with the death. Some children, especially adolescents, believe that keeping their emotions in check is the grown-up thing to do. By contrast, parents are often eager to help their child enter into a discussion of grief.

It is common for children to have feelings of guilt connected with the loss in their life. The fact is, some adolescents are not interested in exploring their bereavement process, especially if their parent is insisting, hovering, or pleading for such a move. Suggestions follow for parents who feel that their children need help. However, be aware that, despite what parents want, the child may simply refuse to discuss feelings of grief in general and guilt in particular.

Don't force or use heavy emotional pleas. Most children report that they find it very difficult to handle their parents' emotional upset. In addition, when a grandchild has died, grandparents find it very difficult as they mourn the death and at the same time feel guilty and helpless watching their own child in excruciating pain. For parents and grandparents, here are examples of helpful outlets.

- Inform the teacher and school counselor of the death.
- Talk to your child about your own guilt. It may help your child to feel more free to discuss his or her guilt.
- Purchase a book on bereavement for young people.
- Search for a youth grief group.
- Say to the child, "Sometimes when a person dies, we might think it's because of something we said or we did or didn't do…Have you ever felt that way?" Then, be silent and listen.
- Ask an admired older friend or relative who understands youth and grief to discuss the loss with your child.
- Involve your child in the next holiday in which the person who died will be acknowledged.
- Watch for and take advantage of teachable moments in which a news event, movie, or relevant situation can serve as a catalyst for discussion.

• Be patient with your child's bereavement process. Certainly address any emotional or behavioral problems by getting needed help, but realize that your child may not focus on the loss and grief until months or years later.

About one-third of the students who take my death education college course had lost a sibling or parent anywhere from a few weeks to several decades earlier! One woman in her mid-thirties said to me that she took the course to explore the suicide of her father 30 years earlier. She stated, "I wasn't ready to go into depth about my father's suicide in my childhood or even in my twenties. But now I think I'm ready." (She was.)

9. Thought-Stopping

Thought-Stopping is a technique that counselors have used to help a person who is having problems with obsessive, intrusive thoughts that disrupt his or her life. A man whose son died in a motorcycle accident had recurring thoughts of a voice in his head saying, "You bought the bike. You knew it was dangerous."

This thought became so disruptive that the man had a difficult time concentrating at work. In counseling, the man was told:

> In a minute I will want you to think about the disruptive thought. As soon as the thought comes fully into your mind, raise your index finger. At that very instant I will yell 'STOP!' in a loud and sharp voice. It will be loud enough to startle you; but you may notice that the thought is disrupted and may quickly fade away or at least decrease in intensity.

You do not necessarily need a counselor to help you with this. You can have a friend help by showing him or her how to do it. An alternative method that may be effective is for you to tell yourself "STOP!" The important thing is for "STOP!" to be sudden and very loud so that it disrupts the thought pattern. It is not a cure-all, but it can help. If, after trying this, your intrusive thoughts continue, consider having a counselor assist you.

10. Understand that feeling less guilt does not mean that you are letting go of your loved one.

I discussed this a few pages back. This is one of the most important facts that you must come to realize: getting better, feeling less guilt, and beginning to enjoy life does not mean that you are forgetting your loved one. Your goal, then, is to find ways to hold this person in your heart while you are beginning to feel a little better. To help with this, see the next suggestion: Compiling Memories.

11. Compiling memories

One of the contributing factors to some types of guilt is the fear or concern that our loved one will be forgotten. This was mentioned earlier in the section on Getting Better Guilt. Support groups, books, and hobby shops can provide a number of suggestions for compiling memories.

Here are a few:
a. Put together a picture album story of the person's life.
     Contact friends and relatives to obtain pictures.
b. Same as above, but ask about video or audiotapes.
c. Write stories or record on tape the stories about the person
     who died. It can be called "I remember the time when . . . ."
     It is a wonderful way to compile a number of stories into
     one place. When you call friends and relatives to ask them
     for pictures and videos, also ask them to think of a story.
     Make an appointment for a 15-minute interview; or if you
     have voice mail, you can ask to record their story over the
     phone.
d. Send out emails on your loved one's birthday, asking for stories.

Be aware that some people may not want to participate in your project. Try not to let that stop you from continuing. In accordance with Suggestion #2, Focus on the Positive, this project can help you relive some positive experiences in the life of your loved one.

12. A chat with my loved one

This is an exercise some people find difficult to do. So, please be ready for what may be an explanation of a highly emotional experience. In this exercise I am asking you to imagine that your loved one is going to visit you for 20 seconds. The question you are going to hear being answered by this person is, "What do you have to say to me about the guilt that I've been carrying since your death?"

Now, please imagine your loved one standing in front of you answering this question. Even if this person is a baby, imagine receiving a message from him or her. Listen. What words do you hear?

Next, take out a pen and paper and write these words. Understand that this is a gift that your loved one has given you. Accept the gift.

If, however, the message that you received was negative, for example, "You should feel guilty," your best response to it could be, "I will not let you control me after death." Therefore, this experience can work for you either way.

An example of a negative message occurred with 21 year-old Tina whose father died when she was 18. He had always wanted her to attend college and become a teacher. However, Tina had no interest in going to college and was happy with her job as a grocery cashier. Whenever she heard any reference to college or to teaching, she experienced feelings of anxiety, knowing that she was defying her father's wishes. When she imagined her father speaking to her, his words were, "Why aren't you following my last wish, Tina?" Tina was able to reply, "Dad, I know you meant well. But this is my life and I am living it the way I want. I know that, wherever you are, that's what you would really want for me."

An example of a positive message occurred when a 31 year-old man, Yuri, worked on the guilt he felt for not visiting his ill grandmother in the nursing home during the last year of her terminal illness. When he imagined her in front of him, the words he heard were, "Yuri, I know that you love me and not visiting me at that time in my life is completely understandable. Remember, Grandma has always loved you. Now, do what Grandma says and stop punishing yourself." The morning after hearing his grandmother's words, Yuri reported that he awakened and felt "somehow lighter, not knowing why," until he remembered his experience the previous day. He stated, "It's only been a few days now but I know this great feeling has to be related to the lifting of the incredible guilt I'd been carrying for over a year!"

Now that you've read this suggestion, and before you go to the next page, I invite you to put down this book and go through this exercise. I have done this in guilt workshops with hundreds of people; and most find this a highly moving and meaningful experience. Are you willing to try?

13. Self-forgiveness
For many people, self-forgiveness is ultimately at the heart of their guilt work. Forgiving does not mean forgetting. Definitions of forgive from the dictionary [25] include phrases such as:
>   to give up resentment
>   to grant relief from payment
>   allow room for error or weakness.

Unless you can find a way to begin to forgive yourself, the other suggestions in this book will probably not have the positive effect they might otherwise have had.

Answer the following questions: What would it take for me to forgive myself? Write out your answer. What did you say? Was it realistic? Is there anything you can do now to begin this process? Whenever you catch yourself in the guilt mode, this can be a helpful question to get you back on track. Perhaps you can engage in some positive form of actual or symbolic restitution, such as writing a letter to your loved one. Some people who have done this have found it helpful to follow up with a reply letter from their loved one. This can be especially helpful if you have unfinished business with this person.

In his book *Who Dies* [26] Stephen Levine urges readers to go deep within their hearts and say, "I forgive you." I ask you to do the same. Let the words come from your lips—in a whisper if you must—but say them. Let the meaning begin to fill your chest and to flow throughout your body. Don't be scared. Feel it. It is OK to do this.

By forgiving yourself you will not forget the lessons you have learned. It is important for you, as Levine says, to soften. Let yourself do this as you permit forgiveness to melt some of the hardness that has built up. At various times during the next several days and months bring the words again to your lips, "I forgive you."

14. The best friend approach

In this approach you are asked to imagine that your best friend, rather than you, is in the same situation. You are now about to give your own words of wisdom regarding the guilt your best friend has been feeling. What words come to mind? Say them in mind right now as you read this.

Now, can you take those same words and say them to yourself? What I am obviously asking you to do is try to treat yourself as you would treat your best friend. This task might be difficult for you. But, reach out, take your own hand and be kind and gentle to yourself. As much as you might feel that you don't "deserve" such gentle treatment, again ask yourself, "What would I say to my best friend?" And then say it to yourself.

15. Write a list of all you did wrong and all you did right with this person.

This is related to Suggestion #4, Focus on the Positives: but this time we are looking at both sides. We're still waiting for the perfect parent, the model spouse, the flawless brother or sister. Of course you did things wrong with this person. List every one of them. Once you've completed that list, write out all the things you did right with this person. It's so easy to beat yourself up and focus on the negatives; but you must also look at the positives. If you were a child when your loved one died, respect the fact that kids say and do all kinds of things. So, be ready to forgive the words and deeds of a child (you), OK?

Please pick up your pen or go to your computer and write. Once you get going you'll see what I mean. One other related step in this exercise is to write out all the things you wish you had done differently and next to each underline the good intentions.

16. Work on identifying, reducing, and eliminating any form of self-punishment

Take out a sheet of paper, date it, and answer the following questions on guilt and self-punishment:

a. How have I punished myself?

b. How have I permitted others to punish me?

c. When I punish myself or leave it to others, what am I thinking at the time?

d. For what reason(s) have I punished myself?

e. In punishing myself, am I also hurting anyone else?

   If your answer to this question is "no," is it possible that your behavior is affecting someone else in a way that you are not aware? Who might it be?

f. Am I willing to let go of some or all of these self-punishing behaviors? If yes then:

   (1) Exactly what am I willing to commit to do today?

   (2) On what day am I willing to begin?

   (3) What would it feel like if I never self-punished again?

If you are ready to commit, are you willing to write out your commitment? It can say something like this:

"Out of love and respect for my loved one _____, I commit to stop punishing myself in the following ways_____
_____."

17. Role-taking

Perhaps you are not ready to let go of your guilt feelings. Consider this: Live the next five minutes of your life "as if" you were guilt-free. Do this so that you can experience what it would feel like, but with the understanding that you can go back to your original guilt feelings anytime you want. People who have tried this have stated that it takes away the uncomfortable feeling of suddenly trying to let go of the guilt they've carried for so long.

Are you ready to try it? Here are the steps:

a. If you begin to catch yourself saying any guilt-related statements, stop your negative self-talk and say to yourself, "It's OK. For now I am putting aside my guilt. That's it, just let it go." And see if you can sustain a guiltless five-minute interval. Go to step b.

b. Don't be hard on yourself if you don't do it perfectly. You are giving yourself some important practice and proving to yourself that you are able to do this for a period of time.

c. If you are able to reach the five-minute point, try it again later for 15 minutes.

d. See if you can actually work up to a full day. One entire day without guilt. Try it just to see what it feels like.

Remember, you can return to your guilt anytime you want.

18. Setting a date

This is similar to the Role-Taking exercise. However, in this case you are to pick a date in the future when you will commit -- from that day forward -- to changing your guilt self-talk.

Some people choose the anniversary date of their loved one's death. Other people choose their own birthday (as a type of birthday present from the person who died) or the birthday of their loved one or some other meaningful day.

If you feel like this sounds like a good idea, write the following statement and put it in a place where you can see it daily: "I'm going to change my guilt self-talk on the following date: _____. I will say the following no more: _____ _____"and "What I can do now is_____."

19. Spiritual approach

Have a conversation with God or with some other supreme being. Or write a letter. Some people believe that God punishes the guilty and subsequently they become angry with God for that. As I discussed in the section on the Spiritual Dimension of Guilt, it takes some people a while before they can restore their relationship with God.

If you have a belief in God and are ready, you may want to express all your guilt feelings in prayer and engage in a conversation with Him. Ask, "God, what do you say about guilt? About forgiveness? About my carrying this guilt around for this length of time?"

You may want to discuss your guilt with your spiritual advisor and examine your belief about a punitive deity. It also may help if you consult your spiritual book to read passages on guilt and forgiveness.

20. Individual and group support

Some people work on their grief and guilt alone, some do it with another person or two, and some find a group setting is helpful. Do you have one or more persons in your life who can be a good listener to you without judgment? This is especially helpful if you are dealing with any difficult guilt issues such as Unmentionable Guilt. Who is this person? If you haven't done so already, have you made contact?

There are grief support groups in most communities throughout the United States and Canada and on the Internet. People in these groups have experienced a loss similar to yours. Call the local crisis center, mental health facility, church, hospital, hospice, or funeral home to find support in your area. It makes no difference whether you are recently bereaved or it has been decades.

A support group can offer you informational and emotional support. Many people who join report that, after a few meetings, they feel comfortable in sharing some of the more difficult parts of their grief reactions.

Support group members report that they have been able to say things to the group that they felt they could never say to their family.

For example, one man whose 30 year-old daughter had died from a drug overdose, was able to say to his support group, "I've never been able to say this to anyone before, but I feel that if she had continued to live, she would have gotten into even more trouble and caused more heartache both for herself and our family." Once this man said this, he reported that a burden had been lifted.

21. Performing a Ritual

Some of the contributors to this book stated that performing a ritual has been helpful in easing their guilt. One woman, whose sister had died from suicide, stated that each person in her support group was asked to go around and state which aspect of guilt they were ready to let go of. She stated:

> When it got to me, I was scared, I'm not sure why. But I managed to say that I was letting go of the guilt I felt for not realizing how much emotional pain my sister was in when she took her life. After I walked out of the meeting and for the past eight months since I said it, I have felt that this aspect of my guilt is one less thing I've had to worry about.

Another woman, whose son died in combat, shared a story of lighting a "guilt candle" in her support group for bereaved parents. She stated that when she blew out the candle as she thought about the guilt she felt for letting her son join the military, it felt like a weight had been lifted from her shoulders.

A similar ritual involves writing your guilt issues on a piece of paper, then wadding it up and throwing it in the fireplace.

In the Guilt workshop I give I pass out small, polished rocks to each audience member telling them it is their Guilt Rock; and after the workshop they need to decide whether they are ready to throw it away or take it home. If they take it home they decide how close to their side they want to keep the rock, for example carrying it in their purse or pocket or keeping it on their night stand. As the days and weeks turn into months, they may want to move the rock further away, perhaps putting it outside and eventually taking it someplace and throwing it away.

22. Channeling guilt

One way that people cope with the incredible guilt they feel is to channel it into a worthwhile project. This does not mean that any project pursued by a bereaved person is necessarily a result of guilt. Often it is not. The ability to give to another person or to a cause without expecting something in return is a tribute to the human spirit. It helps answer the question, "What can I do now?"

Ask yourself :

> Into what kind of project, activity, or work can I
> channel my guilt?
> How might I serve my community to honor my loved one?
> What organization would appreciate my volunteer work?
> How can I raise funds for a good cause?
> What can I create?
> What can I build?

Summary

As a summary of all I have discussed here I want to share with you a personal experience and a poem that captures much of what I am suggesting in this book. In 1987 I was asked to serve as a member of the advisory board of the King County (Seattle) chapter of The Compassionate Friends, a bereaved parents' organization. I was honored to be the only nonbereaved parent to serve on the board. A few years later I attended a retreat with the committee to plan the next year's agenda. It's my job to provide input, when needed, from the perspective of a nonbereaved parent.

At the end of a long Saturday meeting the group looked at me, and said, "OK, Dr. Bob, what do you have to say about all this?" I had been taking notes and had found myself putting them in the form of a poem. I gave my feedback by reading the poem. The group was moved as they heard their story put before them. I offer it to you on the next page as an inspirational example of working with your own grief while helping others:

Saturday

On a Saturday in Fall
I am sitting at a long table in a house
amidst trees, rain, fog
Around this table sits a group of 15 people
Human beings who have lived and are living a terrible nightmare
the death of a child
But, amazingly, they are not here to mourn, but to give
Not to isolate, but to bond
Not to take, but to share
Not to cry, but they can
Long ago, when first asked to sit at this table,
each replied, "Not me, I don't think I'm ready."
But all agreed today at this table
it is a way to give
a way to give back
The talk today is of planning future ways of giving to others
facilitator training, newsletters, retreats, phone call support,
mailings, parent meetings, fund raising, facing the holidays,
regional and national conferences, and more meetings
All this is focused on the parents who will come after them
And they remember the fragility, the confusion, the craziness
With these feelings at the forefront
decision upon decision eventually emerges fully crafted.

At thousands of homes across Seattle on this Saturday in Fall
people rake leaves, shop,
listen to the Huskies, and catch up on chores
But here, in a living room at a long table,
fifteen parents, each with a child taken from them,
give.

Conclusion

You have chosen to work on one of the most difficult issues in the bereavement process. By looking at guilt from a number of perspectives, I hope you have learned much about this complex grief reaction. You may have seen yourself in descriptions of the guilt behaviors, such as guilt self-talk, obsessive thoughts, and inflexible rituals. You should now be able to identify how defense mechanisms, selective perception, and guilt schema are related to guilt. Your awareness of the way you punish yourself and your ability to identify the various types of guilt have hopefully given you new insight. The suggestions for coping have given you some tools to use whenever you are ready.

Remember, each situation is different and you decide when you are ready to let go of any part of your guilt at your pace, your time. No one can make this decision for you. Finally, I would like to say that, as you move through your guilt and grief, please be gentle and kind to yourself and to the people around you. Many of the thousands of bereaved people I have worked with during the past 30 years believed that they couldn't make it another day. Yet, they did.

With warmest regards,

Bob Baugher

About The Author

Bob Baugher, Ph.D. is a Psychology Instructor at Highline Community College near Seattle where he teaches courses in Death Education, Human Relations, Suicide Intervention, Human Sexuality, and Understanding AIDS. As a certified death educator and counselor he has worked with bereaved parents, siblings, spouses, and children who have lost parents. His doctoral dissertation is entitled "Perceptions of the Widow's Bereavement Process by her Adult Child." Since 1987, he has served on the advisory board for the King County Chapter of The Compassionate Friends. As a clinician Bob has co-facilitated children's grief support groups and worked on a three-year research project with the University of Washington entitled The Parent Bereavement Project. He has written six other books and has given more than 500 workshops on grief and loss.

References

[1] Morris, W. (Ed.) (1971). *American Heritage Dictionary of the English Language.* Boston: Houghton Mifflin Co., 585.

[2] Esser, A. (1974). In A. Deeken, *Process and Permanence in Ethics: Max Scheler's Moral Philosophy.* New York: Paulist Press.

[3] Kohner, N. & Henley, A. (2001). *When a Baby Dies: The Experience of Late Miscarriage, Stillbirth, and Neonatal Death.* London, England: Routledge, p. 74.

[4] Barr, P. & Cacciatore, J. (2007-2008). Problematic emotions and maternal grief. *Omega, 56*(4), 331-348.

[5] Rando, T. (1986). (Ed.). *Parental Loss of a Child.* Champaign, IL: Research Press Co.

[6] Gilbert, R.B. (2003). *Guilt and Shame: The Human Experience.* Presentation for The University of Texas Health Science Center at San Antonio Teleconference Network of Texas.

[7] Labrum, D. & Gloster, M. (2005). *The Hole in Me Since the Day You Died.* South Bend IN: The Center for Hospice and Palliative Care, Inc.

[8] Camile, N. The Neuro-science of regret, *Science,* May 21, 2004, p. 1116-1117.

[9] Miles, M.S. & Demi, A.S., (1986). Guilt in bereaved parents. In T. Rando (Ed.). *Parental Loss of a Child.* Champaign, IL: Research Press Co., 97-118.

[10] Baugher, B. & Sims, D. (2007). *The Crying Handbook.* Newcastle, WA: Caring People Press.

[11] Martin, K. (1998). *When a Baby Dies of SIDS.* Edmonton, Alberta: Qual Institute Press.

[12] Veerman, D. & Barton, B. (2003). *When Your Father Dies: How a Man Deals with the Loss of a Father.* Nashville, TN: Thomas Nelson, Inc., pp. 23-24.

[13] Schiff, H.S. (1983). *The Bereaved Parent.* NY: Penguin Books, p. 37.

References

[14] DeFrain, J. Martens, L. Stork, J. & Stork, W. (1990-91). The psychological effects of a stillbirth on surviving family members. *Omega, 22*(2), 81-108.

[15] Sanders, D.M. (1992). *Surviving Grief and Learning to Live Again*, NY: John Wiley and Sons, p. 63.

[16] Elison, J. & McGonigle, C. (2004), *Liberating Losses: When Death Brings Relief.* Cambridge, MA: Lifelong Books.

[17] Baugher, R. (Jan-Feb, 1995). What if I Grieved Perfectly? *Bereavement Magazine*, p. 14-15.

[18] Boss, P. (Dec, 2002). Ambiguous loss in families of the missing. *The Lancet, 380*, S39-40.

[19] Pennebaker, J.W. (1997). *Opening up: The healing power of expressing emotions.* New York: Guilford.

[20] Murphy, S.A., Johnson, L.C. & Lohan, J. (2003). Finding meaning in a child's violent death: A five-year prospective analysis of parents' personal narratives and empirical data. *Death Studies, 27(5)*, 381-404.

[21] Golden, T.R. (1996). *Swallowed by a Snake: The Gift of the Masculine Side of Healing.* Kensington, MD: Golden Healing Publishing L.L.C., p. 68.

[22] Freeman, A. & DeWolf, R. (1989). *Woulda, Coulda, Shoulda.* NY: HarperCollins.

[23] Baugher, B. & Jordan, J. (2002). *After Suicide Loss: Coping with Your Grief.* Newcastle, WA: Caring People Press.

[24] Rack, J.J., Burleson, B.R., Bodie, G.D., Holmstrom, A.J., & Servaty-Seib, H. (2008). Bereaved adults' evaluations of grief management messages: Effects of message person centeredness, recipient individual differences, and contextual factors. *Death Studies, 32*, 399-427.

[25] *Webster's Universal Encyclopedic Dictionary.* (2002). NY: Merriam-Webster, Inc.

[26] Levine, S. (1982). *Who Dies?* Garden City, NY: Anchor Books.

Acknowledgments

There are many people to thank for their valuable contributions in helping to make this book a reality. Their input on drafts of the first and second editions of this book helped to shape this final product. I have placed their names following the Reference section because for me they were essential resources. Thanks to all of you:

Sue Anderson
Shawn Baugher
Karyl Chastain Beal
John Bell
Mary McCampbell Bell
Lois Bloom
Donna Borman
Karen Brown
Jessica Carlson
Amelia Carroll
Linda Coughlin
Barbe Creagh
John Dittmer
Marilyn Evans
Linda Wong Garl
Helen Godwin
Yola Hauskins
Danny Hodges
Bob Keene
Rich Klepac
Carl Komor

Virginia Kozlowski
Mary Ann Mathis
Michael McDowell
Denise Montoya
Sara Montz
Dennis Moyers
Penny Penland
Ann Marie Putter
John Schmeelk
Floyd Schwanz
Becky Sharpe
Darcie Sims
Bill Snapp
Margarita Suarez
Carol Sunada
Diane Twitty
Sara Weiss
Dennis Williams
Barbara Zick
Amanda Zurwell

Thanks to my daughter, Janée Baugher, MFA, for her insightful editorial input.

Thanks also go to my wife, Kris, for her love, support, suggestions, and for her many hours of computer and production work in preparing this book for publication.

DISCOUNTS FOR ORDERING MULTIPLE COPIES OF GUILT DURING BEREAVEMENT

2-10 copies	5% Discount
11-24 copies	10% Discount
25-49 copies	20% Discount
50-99 copies	30% Discount
100 or more	35% Discount

Price: $10.00 (U.S. funds) per copy
Add $2.00 postage for a single copy
Free postage for U.S. orders of 2 or more copies
Shipping: Canadian and out of U.S. orders will be billed according to postal rates.

WASHINGTON STATE RESIDENTS ADD 9.5% SALES TAX
Please allow 2-4 weeks for delivery

Send Check or Money Order to:
Bob Baugher, Ph.D.
7108 127th Place SE
Newcastle, WA 98056-1325
or
email your order and you will be billed
b_kbaugher@yahoo.com

OTHER BOOKS BY DR. BOB BAUGHER:

- *A Guide for the Bereaved Survivor* with Marc Calija
- *The Crying Handbook* with Darcie Sims
- *Understanding Anger during Bereavement* with Carol and Gary Hankins
- *Death Turns Allie's Family Upside Down* with Linda Wong-Garl and Kristina J. Baugher
- *Coping with Traumatic Death: Homicide* with Lew Cox
- *After Suicide: Coping with Your Grief* with Jack Jordan

Pricing and taxes subject to change without notice